Audrey's Journey — Loving Kindness

By Kerry Alison Wekelo

Illustrations by Irene Olds

Dedicated to Rolf Gates — a true inspiration in my journey

Published by Peaceful Daily

ISBN: 978-0-9884926-3-9 (hard cover)
978-0-9982579-1-4 (ebook)

Library of Congress Control Number: 2016946849

Any people depicted in stock imagery provided by Thinkstock are models,
and such images are being used for illustrative purposes only.

Certain stock imagery © Thinkstock.

Prepress by Perseus-Design.com

This book is printed on acid-free paper.

Audrey has a love for music and creating rhymes on her drum. When Audrey plays her drum she is filled with love and happiness.

In this journey, Audrey envisions how Metta Meditation can help to spread love and kindness to all living things.

Hi! I am Audrey. I love to come up with happy rhymes with my drum.

Dum ditty,
dum ditty,
dum dum,
dum . . .

Ah, Metta meditation.

Can you say that three times really fast?

Metta meditation.

Metta meditation.

Metta meditation.

Metta is a way to offer love and happiness to ourselves, to people we love, and to all living creatures.

To offer Metta, you first offer yourself loving kindness and then to someone you love like your mom or dad. The last step is to offer love and happiness to everyone.

Let's try together. Repeat after me:

May I be safe.
May I be happy.
May I be peaceful.
May I be healthy.
May I walk with love in my heart.

May my mom be safe.
May my mom be happy.
May my mom be peaceful.
May my mom be healthy.
May my mom walk with love in her heart.

May my dad be safe.
May my dad be happy.
May my dad be peaceful.
May my dad be healthy.
May my dad walk with love in his heart.

May we be safe.
May we be happy.
May we be peaceful.
May we be healthy.
May we walk with love in our hearts.

Books by Kerry

Audrey's Journey – Round and Round Yoga

Blaine's Playful Namaste

If It Does Not Grow Say No – Eatable Activities for Kids

Let's Do Yoga – Coloring and Activity Book

Pile of Smile Activity Book

www.ingramcontent.com/pod-product-compliance
Lightning Source LLC
Chambersburg PA
CBHW060755150426
42811CB00058B/1414

Blaine's Playful Namaste

ustrated by:

rene Olds

Kerry Alison Wekelo

Blaine's Playful Namaste

Kerry Alison Wekelo

Illustrated by:
Irene Olds

Published by Peaceful Daily

ISBN: 978-0-9970143-9-6 (hard cover)
978-0-9982579-2-1 (ebook)

Library of Congress Control Number: 2016946852

Any people depicted in stock imagery provided by Thinkstock are models,
and such images are being used for illustrative purposes only.

Certain stock imagery © Thinkstock.

Prepress by Perseus-Design.com

This book is printed on acid-free paper.

Dedicated to Blaine, Ty and Will -
may the light inside you always shine bright.

Special thanks to Will for being the inspiration for this
book with all the daily namaste greetings.

Hi! Our names are Audrey and Blaine. We love to come up with happy rhymes on our drum. One of our favorites is the tune of "Twinkle, Twinkle, Little Star." Do you like that one, too?

Did you know that *namaste* is a greeting that means "I see the light in you, and you see the light in me"?

To perform *namaste*, place your hands together over your heart, close your eyes, and bow your head.

Saying *namaste* is a fun way to honor your friends and family. Where do you think you can say *namaste*? When do you think it might be a good thing to say?

3

Namaste in the morning when you wake up and see the sun.

Namaste in the afternoon when the day is nearly done.

Namaste on the playground when you meet your friends and play.

Namaste during circle time when it's time to
sit and stay.

Namaste with joy at the beauty all around you.

Namaste with love for the miracle that is you.

Namaste with faith the whole day through, for it is the light in me that sees the light in you.

Books by Kerry

Audrey's Journey - Loving Kindness
Audrey's Journey - Round and Round Yoga
If It Does Not Grow Say No - Eatable Activities for Kids
Let's Do Yoga - Coloring and Activity Book
Pile of Smile Activity Book

www.ingramcontent.com/pod-product-compliance
Lightning Source LLC
Chambersburg PA
CBHW060755150426

42811CB00058B/1415